What's Inside

Fight Gravity

Climbing is all about pushing yourself to the limit—physically and mentally.

Imagine yourself clinging to 3,000-foot cliffs, climbing soaring pillars of blue ice, or scaling remote, snow-covered peaks.

Climbing is not just about mountains. There's something for everyone and every level of experience, from boulder climbing and indoor gyms nearby, to lofty heights and wild places on faraway continents.

Just turn these pages, and get ready for some palm-sweating action.

Bouldering

If you want to push your limits without the danger...

If you want to move freely without a lot of complex equipment to weigh you down...

then explore the simple pleasures of pure movement—go bouldering!

Climb
Free

Free climbing is the game most climbers play.

I f you're climbing up rocks without using ropes or equipment to support your weight and help you climb, then you're free climbing. Ropes are often used, but only for safety, and you climb by using only the natural formations of the rock to grab onto and push off from. Free climbing includes sport climbing, traditional (trad) climbing, and bouldering.

LITTLE ROCKS, BIG THRILLS

Bouldering is the simplest form, and the essence of, free climbing—no ropes, no hardware; just rock shoes, chalk, and Mother Nature. It's the perfect entry into the sport of climbing. It can be done on any lump of rock that is low enough to avoid injury in a fall. At its heart, bouldering is pure movement, offering the thrill of gymnastic action with little risk. It's also convenient—wherever there are rocks, there's bouldering—and it can be practiced alone or with a bunch of friends.

Because bouldering often requires doing a series of extremely difficult moves one after the other, some climbers see it as the ideal training for longer, roped climbs. Most people, however, see bouldering as an end in itself—rhythm, power, and plain old fun. Given the lack of equipment and the wide range of movements, bouldering is not only a great beginner's entry into the sport of climbing, but also great training for the cutting-edge climber.

GEAR—THE MINIMALIST

The list of things you'll need for bouldering is as short and simple as the rocks you'll climb.

CHALK BAG: Gymnastic chalk—used to keep the hands dry and tacky—is stored in a drawstring, hand-size pouch and tied around the waist. Most boulderers carry an old toothbrush in the bag to scrub excess chalk off handholds on the rock or to clean dirt and lichen from edges.

CRASH PAD: In bouldering, every fall lands on the ground. Though the falls are usually short, some may be high enough to cause an injury. A crash pad, or foam-cushion mat, keeps those long drops safe and lessens the wear and tear of many short falls.

ROCK SHOES (THE SOLE OF THE CLIMBER): True rock shoes were first used in the 1950s on the world-famous boulders of Fontainebleau near Paris. Those shoes have evolved into today's sensitive, second-skin marvels—so sticky, they act like a second pair of hands.

Modern rock shoes come in two general categories: stiff-soled and soft-soled. Stiff-soled rock shoes, sometimes with a high, ankle-supporting upper, trade sensitivity for sturdiness, making it easier to stand on small rock edges. These shoes have more of a boot-like feel than the popular low-cut, flexible-soled shoes. These flexy slippers allow incredible sensitivity on a wide range of footholds. The fit should be snug—sometimes painfully tight—like the shoes of a ballet dancer. They are covered in super-sticky rubber for maximum grip on the rock.

Small Holds, Big Moves

All the basic movements of rock climbing, including hand and foot positions, are done in bouldering.

Although you can boulder at any difficulty level, the hardest climbing moves in the world are practiced on boulders.

TECHNIQUE

To train for any roped climb, or just to get better at bouldering, here are a few of the key moves to know. Just remember the first rule of climbing: Stay relaxed and focused.

DYNO SOAR

Imagine arriving close to the top of a difficult boulder climb and finding the final handhold hopelessly out of reach. You try everything, but still come up several inches short. It's time for an all-out airborne lunge—the dynamic movement, or "dyno." This move is one of the most useful in all of free climbing and, because it's risky, should be practiced first on boulders.

A dyno uses the body's momentum to reach holds that would otherwise be too far to grab. Dynos can also be the most efficient way to move between holds that are barely within reach.

DOING THE DYNO

1. Straighten your arms, and lower your body onto your feet.
2. Concentrate and exhale as you lunge.
3. Push yourself upward with your feet, not your arms.
4. Focus on catching the hold without overshooting.

SPOTTING

The spotter helps the other climber by breaking his or her fall, or by redirecting the climber to a spotting pad or a flat landing. The spotter stands behind the boulderer, ready to support and redirect him or her. Don't try to catch the climber, or you'll end up crushed like a bug. A good spotter can make the difference between a successful ascent and a broken leg—or worse. Spotting is a very serious responsibility.

Keep a few things in mind:
• Protect the climber's head and back.
• Spot with arms extended and thumbs tucked.
• On vertical rock, catch the climber by the hips and direct him or her to a pad or safe landing.
• On overhangs, catch the climber under the arms so his or her feet strike the ground first.
• If the landing is rocky, *push* the falling climber towards a crash pad or safe, clear zone.

FALLING

Remember that falling is an art in itself. Practicing how to fall is as important as practicing how to climb. Being aware of your positioning before and during a fall can save you from breaking a bone.

Some tips:
• Try to remain poised and upright in a fall.
• Work on those catlike reflexes. Practice being able to land lightly on your feet.

Talk It

Free climbing has a language all its own. Knowing some of the terms—especially the more technical ones—is essential.

Being able to communicate quickly and precisely with your climbing partner or spotter can make a climb easier and faster, or save you from an injury. That's why a climbing word seems to have developed for every technique, bolt, and crag. You'll see some useful terms on these pages.

BOULDERING AND FREE CLIMBING GLOSSARY

BETA: Refers to the old Betamax videos and means memorized route sequences, tricks, or techniques. A generic term for any useful route information.

BUCKET: A large, secure handhold that's a natural formation of the rock, shaped like the lip of a bucket. Also called a "jug."

CRIMP: An edge so small, fingertips must be stacked on top of each other to hold onto it. "Crimping" is the act of climbing small edges. "Crimpy" describes a section of rock with many crimp holds.

CRUX: The hardest move or series of moves on a route.

PUMPED: When muscles—usually in the forearms—swell from being pushed too hard. This often happens right before the climber falls off.

DEADPOINT: During a dyno, when a hold is caught at the top point of the lunge, it's the moment before the body begins to fall backwards—the point when you feel weightless.

EDGING: Standing carefully on tiny footholds.

HEEL HOOK: An ape-like maneuver where you place a heel high—sometimes above your head—to support weight. Also used around corners or on holds for balance.

HIGHBALL: A boulder problem high enough, or with a landing bad and jagged enough, to break bones or cause other serious bodily harm. A sharp mental focus, extra pads, extra spotters, or complete avoidance will keep you intact.

JAMMING: Wedging body parts—including fingers, hands, fists, toes, and feet—into cracks.

LAYBACK: To pull on a vertical hold or crack with the hands while the feet push against the rock in the opposite direction. Also called a "lieback."

MANTEL: To press downward with one or both palms on a ledge or hold to raise the body, so a foot can be placed on the same hold or ledge.

MATCHING: Placing both hands, or both feet, on the same hand or foothold.

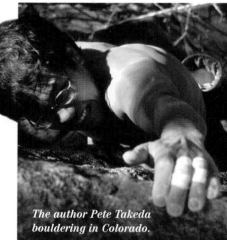

The author Pete Takeda bouldering in Colorado.

MONO: A small hole or pocket in a rock face, just large enough to insert a single finger.

OVERHANG: A face of the rock above that slopes toward you. Can be merely steep or completely horizontal like a ceiling.

PROBLEM: A climbing route. It got its name because figuring out the moves is like solving a puzzle.

PROJECT: A climb or boulder problem that takes repeated days' effort to ascend successfully.

SEND: To complete a successful ascent. Example: "Dude, send that boulder problem."

SIDE PULL: A vertical handhold.

SLAB: A less-than-vertical sheet of rock, usually at a low angle between 45 and 70 degrees.

SLOPER: A hold or feature on a rock lacking a distinct edge. Slopers are climbed using hand or foot friction.

SMEAR: A footwork technique where the climber slides the sole of the shoe across the rock. The friction helps you stick.

STEM (OR STEMMING): To spread out the feet on opposing holds.

TRAVERSE: To climb sideways.

UNDERCLING: To grab the underside of an upside-down hold.

WIRE: To memorize a sequence move by move.

Boulder Problem Solver

If you like to climb rocks, it's hard not to love bouldering. Just pick a rock and go.

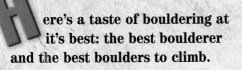 ere's a taste of bouldering at it's best: the best boulderer and the best boulders to climb.

Chris Sharma climbing Realization.

CHRIS SHARMA

On July 18, 2001, in Ceuse, France, 20-year-old Chris Sharma, one of the world's top boulderers, completed a four-year mission: to be the first to free climb a 120-foot-long (37-m) rock climb he named Realization, which has a difficulty level higher than any previously attempted free climb. To train for it, Sharma roped up only once in the two years before the climb. The rest of his time was spent bouldering on rocks usually no bigger than a boxcar.

In recent years, Sharma's passion for boulder climbing has spanned Asia, Europe, and his home in California, where he's always conquering tough new boulder problems. He has won competitions and raised the standards of free climbing.

Sharma started climbing at age 11, and by 15 was thought by many to be the best free climber in the world. Never one to take himself too seriously, Sharma says, "Bouldering is a more laid-back approach to climbing. You're just playing on the rocks. It's more fun, and to me that's the most important thing about climbing."

BOULDERING HOTSPOTS

Wherever you live, chances are there is a bouldering area nearby. If there aren't any boulders handy, then you are guaranteed to find some problems in the local climbing gym. The choices of where to boulder are as dizzying as the latest highball you just sent. Here are two hotspots:

HUECO TANKS STATE HISTORIC PARK: Located outside of El Paso, Texas, Hueco Tanks has been called the best bouldering area in the world. Hundreds of iron-hard boulders crowd this two-square-mile (three-square-km) park. Eroded hollows in the rock called "huecos" dot the stone, allowing steep and challenging problems.

FONTAINEBLEAU: Modern bouldering and the modern rock shoe were born on these rocks outside of Paris, France. The area is home to the most fantastic collection of sandstone boulders in the world.

Sport Climbing

You're a hundred feet (30 m) up, with arms turning to jelly. You dyno for the next edge, but try as you may, you can't hold it. You're airborne, and the ground rushes towards you. All of a sudden, you spring up through the air like a bungee jumper, and you're bobbing on the rope, having grazed nothing but air. That's the fun, safe rush of sport climbing.

Go Sport!

Sport climbing is the most widely practiced form of roped free climbing.

Sport climbing is outdoor free climbing using ropes only for safety—not to support or help in the climb—and metal studs, called bolts, that are already placed in the rock.

STEEP THRILLS

When the rocks are tall enough that you need ropes for safety, there are two options—sport and traditional (trad) climbing. Both require a partner and equipment. The climbers wear harnesses and are tied to a rope. The leader clips equipment onto the anchors in the rock to safeguard his or her climbing progress. The follower, or second, feeds the rope out, or "belays," as the leader climbs (see p. 23).

You need a lot of experience climbing and placing hardware if you want to trad climb, but sport climbing bypasses all of that. The routes up the cliff have permanent anchors in the form of bolts. These metal studs are drilled into the rock and placed at convenient locations; they are strong and dependable. The result—the exhilaration of a challenging climb on high, airy cliffs, with the safety of dependable anchors. It's no surprise that the hardest roped climbs in the world are sport climbs.

Sport climbing maximizes the climbing you can do while minimizing the risk. Falling, repeating moves for practice, pulling on equipment, and resting on equipment are all part of the sport climbing game. Wait a minute. Don't these tactics break the definition of free climbing? The answer is, yes they do. But they're allowed in order to practice for an eventual free ascent.

KEY TERMS

EQUIPMENT: The hardware, ropes, and gear used to help you climb.

MULTIPITCH ROUTE: A climb consisting of several belayed (see p. 23) sections of climbing.

PITCH: The stretch of climbing terrain between two belays (see p. 23).

PROTECTION: Protection (or pro, gear) consists of anchors placed into the rock by the leader to reduce the length of the leader's potential fall.

RAPPEL: A rope technique in which the climber slides down a rope using a special device that slows the descent.

RUNNER: A sling connecting the anchor and rope used to decrease extra weight from rope drag on the leader.

RUNOUT: The distance between the leader and the last anchor. The leader will fall twice the distance he or she has climbed above the most recent runner—often a frightening experience. A long runout means a potentially long fall.

FREE ASCENTS

REDPOINT: A bottom-to-top free ascent that's accomplished after you've rehearsed it, figured out the route and moves, and practiced it segment by segment.

FLASH: A bottom-to-top free ascent completed on the first try with some prior knowledge of sequences and strategy.

ON-SIGHT FLASH: A bottom-to-top free ascent completed on the first try with no prior knowledge of the route.

Know the Ropes

Sport climbing can be a thrill, but you won't get more than a few feet unless you know what to do.

These terms and techniques will help you out and teach you how to fall—the right way.

DON'T FEAR THE WHIP

Failure is a constant companion to those who push their limits. In sport climbing, to fall, or "whip," is not only common, it's necessary for true success. You'll never discover your limits unless you exceed them. The fear of falling is one of the greatest obstacles to sport climbing success.

We don't like to fall. Plummeting through space while trusting your life to a thin nylon rope is not the easiest thing to do. But if you want to reach your potential, you've got to learn to fall. Practice falling from higher and higher points above the last bolt. Go to the local climbing gym and take whippers in a safe, controlled, indoor environment.

FOR THOSE ABOUT TO FALL

- Maintain body control by trying to stay upright.
- Stay relaxed.
- Avoid tangling the rope in your legs, which can flip you upside down, causing you to hit your head.
- Try hard! Fall off while going for the next move, not because you let go.

KEY TERMS

ANCHORS: Anchors include trees, spikes of rock, hardware placed by the climber in cracks, and permanent fixtures such as bolts—anything a climber uses to hold his or her body (or the rope) to the climbing surface.

BELAY: To belay a climber is to safeguard them using a rope. If the leader, or "climber," falls, the second or, "belayer," will hold them with the rope. The entire system (at right) is called "the belay"

LEAD: To lead is to climb first, placing or clipping protection on the way up. Leading demands taking charge of your own safety. It is the ultimate roped climbing experience—the risks are sometimes high, but the rewards are great.

TOPROPE: Toprope climbing is climbing with a secure overhead belay rope set up in a slingshot fashion.

FOLLOWER: The follower, or "second or belayer," climbs the pitch after the leader. The second usually cleans the pitch—removing hardware placed by the leader.

Anchor

TOPROPE CLIMB

Belay device (see p. 25)

Locking carabiner (see p. 25)

Climber

Belay device and carabiner

Belayer

23

Equipment

The sport climber's gear is simple, light, and built for performance.

he right gear maximizes your comfort and minimizes risk. You'll be the first one up the rock face, and you'll stay safe.

BUILT FOR FLIGHT

ROPE: The rope is a climber's lifeline. A climbing rope has the stretch of a bungee cord and the strength of steel cable. Modern climbing ropes are made up of a twisted or braided core of elastic fibers covered by a woven protective nylon sheath. The standard diameter sport (and trad) climbing rope is 10 to 11 millimeters (about .4 in.), although some climbers choose thinner ropes. These aren't as durable, but they weigh less. The standard rope length is 50 meters (165 feet), but 60 meters (200 feet) is rapidly becoming the norm.

CARABINER: A metal device that quickly connects gear together (see picture, p. 23).

RUNNERS: Two carabiners joined by a sewn nylon or synthetic fiber sling is called a runner. A runner lets the rope run smoothly and allows the climber to quickly attach the rope to an anchor. The sport climber's runner of choice is called a quickdraw.

HARNESS: A climbing harness consists of a waist belt and leg loops sewn from flat, woven, nylon webbing. Modern harnesses are padded with synthetic fleece and/or molded foam. Sport harnesses are simple and lightweight, with a few gear loops for carrying quickdraws.

CHALK BAG: For the sport climber, like the boulderer, chalk (carried in a chalk bag) is essential (see p. 11).

BELAY DEVICE AND LOCKING CARABINER: All climbers who use ropes need an oversized carabiner with a screwgate or locking system so it doesn't accidentally open. This locking carabiner is used in concert with a rope-braking device. The most popular rope brake is the Air Traffic Controller (ATC) type. The rope is threaded through the ATC, then clipped to the locking carabiner. In a fall or rappel (sliding down the rope using a friction device), the device jams the rope and stops it from sliding (see picture, p. 23).

THE HELMET RULE

Any time you tie onto a rope, wear a helmet. Helmets save lives. Whether protecting your head from falling objects or shielding your skull in a fall, a helmet is a necessary investment. Two types are popular—the foam "bike-type" helmet and the hardshell variety. Hard shells take a beating. Foam helmets are lighter and more comfortable but wear out sooner.

CLIP AND GO!

There are hundreds of sport climbing areas worldwide offering great fun on every type and angle of rock. There is most likely a sport climbing cliff in your area. If not, some of the best sport climbing might be found in your local climbing gym. Some noteworthy areas:

SMITH ROCK, OREGON: Smith Rock's pocketed volcanic rock is home to one of the most challenging American rock climbs.

BUOUX AND CEUSE, FRANCE: Steep and flawless limestone with some of the best—and hardest—sport climbs in the world.

THE VERDON GORGE, FRANCE: The Verdon Gorge is comprised of beautiful, climb-ready limestone and contains hundreds of sport routes up to a thousand feet (305 m) long.

Indoor Climbing

Had to be in school all day? Weather bad? No worries. Chances are, there's an indoor climbing gym near you.

With artificial boulders and climbing walls, not only does the gym provide year-round training for the dedicated rock climber, but it also provides a great introduction to the sport.

WALLED IN

In a climbing gym, the surfaces are texturized with holds that are placed by course setters whose job it is to create the routes. Good route-setting is like an art, setting up fun, creative moves that challenge and strengthen the climber.

Most gyms offer classes for beginners just starting out and experienced climbers who want to fine-tune their technique. Gyms usually offer outdoor seminars or classes to those who wish to transfer their indoor skills to natural rock.

The gym is also a great way to meet other climbers and develop partnerships for outdoor climbing. Some indoor walls are constructed in private homes or garages. These walls, although generally smaller, provide the same benefits—the joy of climbing anytime, in any weather.

Trad Climbing

Risk and commitment are
the two cornerstones of the climbing
game. Traditional—or trad—climbing is
the ultimate opportunity to
experience both.

The Head Game

Take your life into your own hands—go trad climbing.

You've been bouldering and climbing sport routes in the gym. You've also done some sport climbing on natural rock. Now it's time for your first traditional, or trad, rock climb.

TRADICAL

Sure, this climb is at a much easier level than the difficult bolted routes you've done. Still, the thought of stopping, wiggling in, and maybe falling on a little wedge doesn't inspire confidence. Nevertheless, you decide to make the next move, exhilarated, adrenalized, and slightly terrified. Welcome to trad climbing.

CHOICES, CHOICES

Trad climbers test themselves on nature's own rock, without sport climbing's gridwork of drilled holes and metal studs. The result—the trad climber must weave an often dangerous path up the raw rock, using only the safeguards he or she creates. It's all about making choices, trusting yourself, and accepting huge amounts of responsibility. This defines the trad climbing experience.

FIND YOUR OWN PATH

Without the comfort of pre-placed bolts, the trad climber must be resourceful, clever, and able to keep a cool head while figuring out the natural rock path. Routes that follow cracks are usually good choices, since they generally offer more opportunities to safeguard yourself. Climbs that offer few protection opportunities require a calm head, nerves of steel, and the maturity to sometimes say "No."

High Gear

Natural gear is what 99 percent of trad climbers use 99 percent of the time.

Natural gear is gear that the climber does not hammer into the rock but rather slings over things like trees or rock spikes. It includes "clean" climbing anchors like wedge-shaped nuts and exotic spring-loaded camming devices (SLCDs) that provide an anchor by being forced into cracks and crevices.

camming device

nut

TRAD GEAR

In addition to the basic equipment of the sport climber, the trad climber must have the experience and ability to effectively place a dizzying array of clean—or un-hammered-in—protection in the rock. On rare occasions, the trad climber will clip into hammered gear such as nail-shaped pitons or bolts. However, hammered gear is the exception rather than the rule.

Throw in a harness with multiple gear loops. Add a pair of high-performance rock shoes comfy enough for all-day use, and you have the gear needed to challenge the rock on its own terms.

TRAD TERMS

AID: To use a piece of equipment to help you climb, or to rest on gear when pumped. Full-on aid climbing is a sport in itself, usually accomplished with heavy-duty equipment on big walls.

BIG WALL: A towering cliff usually exceeding one thousand feet. For an average team of climbers, the length and difficulty of its climb demands a multiday effort.

CRACK CLIMBING: A technique used to ascend a cliff along cracks ranging from fingertip-size to four-foot-wide fissures called chimneys.

EXPOSURE: The psychological and physical sensation of being in a very high, airy, and sensational location.

FACE CLIMBING: Free climbing on protruding edges, pockets, indentations, and huecos (eroded hollows that can range from finger- to bathtub-size). Face climbing sometimes requires only the pure friction of boots and hands on rock.

FIXED GEAR: Gear left permanently in place in the rock. Examples are nylon slings, pitons, and bolts.

GRIPPED: Very frightened.

RACK: Collection of climbing hardware a climber carries, usually clipped by carabiners and arranged on a sling across the chest.

SEW UP: To place many pieces of hardware in a section of rock.

WHERE TO HEAD FOR THE HEAD TRIP

The world is full of great trad climbing crags. Here are a few:

YOSEMITE VALLEY, CALIFORNIA: The world-famous "Valley" holds several lifetimes worth of trad climbing. From the 3,000-foot El Capitan to incredible crack, slab, and face climbing on lesser crags, Yosemite has something for everyone.

ELBSANDSTEINGEBIRGE, GERMANY: These eerie sandstone towers and wall are located near Dresden. Known for long runouts and a clearly defined set of traditional climbing ethics.

SHEFFIELD, ENGLAND: With a long tradition of hard climbing, the Sheffield area offers the traditional climber a great number of options. Most notable are the gritstone crags— short sandstone cliffs with fierce climbing.

El Capitan, Yosemite Valley, California

Big Wall Climbing

Big wall climbs take several days and sometimes weeks to complete.

Big wall climbing takes place on massive cliffs usually exceeding 1,000 feet (305 m). Some big walls have a sheer and almost unbroken expanse of rock for more than 4,000 feet (1,219 m).

BIG TIME

To climb big walls, it's necessary to have a lot of experience in traditional climbing, with extensive knowledge of hardware placement and removal (direct aid), efficient ropework, and route finding. Besides numerous ropes and a huge rack of heavy hardware, big wall climbers must haul days' worth of food, water, and equipment. These supplies, often tipping the scales at several hundred pounds, are packed into durable, bullet-shaped duffel bags and hauled up the wall. A good night's sleep can be found on natural rock ledges, though most big walls are so sheer that a folding, cot-like "portaledge" must be employed. Big wall climbers use extensive direct aid climbing techniques and draw on every trick in the book. Even so, big wall climbing is very dangerous. Some big walls sport long sections of climbing in which gear will barely support human body weight. These sections hold the potential for long and hazardous falls.

GO BIG

EL CAPITAN: At over twice the height of the Empire State Building, El Capitan in California's Yosemite Valley (see picture, p. 33) is the big wall climber's dream. Featuring unbroken sweeps of solid stone up to 3,000 feet (914 m) high, "El Cap" has something for everyone from the big wall novice to the best climbers in the world. Over 70 climbs lace the granite monolith. The famous Nose route—first climbed in 1958—is El Cap's most popular big route. Speed climbers periodically scale the 34-pitch climb in under four hours!

THE ARSENAL

Big walls require specialized gear—and a lot of it. It's a gadget-lover's dream.

AIDERS: Sewn nylon loops in four- to six-step lengths. Used as portable ladders for the aid climber.

ASCENDERS: Also "jumars" or "jugs." These metal clamps are attached to climbing ropes. They slide up but not down, allowing a climber to climb a hanging rope.

COPPERHEADS: Soft copper or aluminum blobs fixed to the end of wire cable loops. The "heads" are mashed with a hammer into grooves or shallow corners in the rock. Copperheads can hold more than the bodyweight of a person.

DAISY CHAIN: Pocketed loops of nylon webbing used to make precise adjustments between the climber and various anchors.

HOOKS: Metal devices (also known as skyhooks or cliffhangers) that hook over flakes, bumps, edges, or holes. Used on the most difficult aid climbs.

hooks

PITONS: Also known as pegs or pins, these nail-like metal spikes are driven into cracks to provide anchors. Pitons range in size and shape from folded metal tacos up to six inches (15 cm) wide, to bird-beak-shaped steel slivers that fit in razor-thin cracks.

pitons

Big League

*There are great climbers, and then there are **great climbers.***

Peter Croft takes risks and succeeds. Lynn Hill is one woman who has performed the impossilble.

Lynn Hill bouldering.

LYNN HILL
AND THE GENDER-FREE NOSE

Rising over 3,000 feet (914 m) from the floor of California's Yosemite Valley, the Nose of El Capitan is perhaps the world's greatest rock climb. Warren Harding, Wayne Merry, and George Whitmore summitted the landmark route in 1958 after 45 days of climbing spread over months. The Nose succumbed to a one-day ascent in 1975. The team of leading Yosemite climbers used extensive equipment and aid techniques. To consider free climbing the Nose was nearly unthinkable. The prevailing attitude of the time was, "No man will ever free the Nose."

So far, no man has. But Lynn Hill did just that in September 1993. To top off her world-class performance, Hill returned the next year and free climbed it in a single day. Despite many unsuccessful efforts by others afterward, the free Nose is, so far, for women only. The petite 40-year-old Hill has also won such events as "The Survival of the Fittest" and more than 30 international competitions, establishing herself as one of the greatest climbers in the world.

PETER CROFT
THE DO-OR-FLY ART OF FREE SOLOING

The term "free soloing" is used to describe the very risky activity of unroped, unprotected climbing. Free soloing is not for the foolhardy. Because it is done on easier climbs and usually only by experienced climbers, the number of free soloing accidents is few. This is a testament to the free soloists' ability, judgement, and restraint. Ask Peter Croft, one of the world's great free climbers and arguably the most accomplished free soloist of all time. "Years ago, I had my first taste of soloing. It was a revelation. It felt dizzyingly close to childhood dreams of flying," he says. "By cranking the volume way down on the difficulty, it felt like gravity took a vacation."

Although he enjoyed the freedom of easier climbs, Croft pushed the standards of free soloing—climbing hard free routes unroped, sometimes over a number of days involving many thousands of feet of climbing. An amazing roped traditional free climber for almost two decades, Croft is perhaps the greatest free solo climber in the world. He's best known for his ascent of Yosemite's notorious Astroman, an 1,100-foot (335-m) granite face of legendary difficulty. The humble Croft insists that free soloing can be safe if practiced by an experienced climber not driven by ego. Restraint and good judgment are the most vital ingredients of the free solo game.

Extreme
Sports

Part 4

Ice Climbing

Winter comes. The air gets cold. Water freezes. A few intrepid climbers embrace this season with gusto, reveling in frozen fingers, harsh winds, and sheer terror. There's nothing like fighting gravity when Nature throws her worst at you. Welcome to the cold, cold world of ice climbing.

The Deep Freeze

Ice is frozen water and, by definition, changeable, brittle, and unreliable stuff.

To the climber, ice poses its own challenges and requires a unique set of tools and techniques.

ICE BOUND

There are many different reasons climbers head for the ice. For some, it allows access to routes on big mountains. For others, ice climbing and its hybrid cousin, mixed climbing, are themselves enough excitement. While the difficulty and danger are real, the jaw-dropping beauty of a crystal blue icescape is worth the practice—and the risk.

ICE CYCLES

Because it's frozen water, ice is continually changing. The same ice climb will vary in difficulty and terrain from year to year and season to season. When the ice first freezes, it is thin and difficult to climb. As the ice thickens, it becomes more reliable and easier to work with.

CHANGING CLIMBS

Temperature also affects the degree of difficulty. When it is extremely cold, the ice becomes brittle, shatters easily, and resists secure ice tool placements. On warmer days, the ice softens, allowing easy and secure pick placements. Popular climbs often become pockmarked from the tools of previous climbers, making the climb easier.

CAUTION ON ICE

Remember—it is up to you to determine how difficult an ice climb really is. Use judgment, be cautious, and take a guidebook difficulty rating as a general suggestion, not gospel. One last thing—don't climb to boast about it later. In ice climbing, an egotistical approach can have serious consequences.

What's the Point?

The point lies in your hands—and on your feet.

Ice climbing is perilous and requires specific equipment to manage the cold, snow, and ice safely.

COLD FEET

Crampons are an erector-set-like framework of metal points attached to your boots with a system of straps and metal-and-plastic bindings. They provide traction in snow and ice, even on relatively steep terrain, and come in two varieties—hinged and rigid. All crampons sport two forward-facing "frontpoints," which allow you to kick into steep and vertical ice.

Hinged crampons are light and flexible, best-used for snow hiking and moderately steep ice climbing, like that of general mountaineering. Heavier, rigid crampons provide a stable platform and are best for steep terrain, such as frozen waterfalls and vertical rock.

PICK-Y

The modern ice climber uses two ice axes. These sinister, hook-shaped implements are called "ice tools." They are usually around a foot-and-a-half long with a rubberized handle and wrist loop. Whether made of aluminum tubing or carbon fiber, most ice tools have a bent shaft with a spike on one end and a toothy, banana-shaped pick on the other. The steel banana pick penetrates ice to help the climber ascend. It is also useful for jamming in rock cracks and hooking rock edges.

MORE ICY GEAR

BOOTS: There are two options—plastic double boots and insulated leather boots. Double boots consist of a foam-insulated inner bootie with a hard plastic shell. Plastics trade flexibility for warmth. Insulated leather boots promise less bulk, better handling, and lighter weight, but they might leave your toes cold.

DOUBLE ROPES: Although not mandatory, two thin ropes used in unison (the double rope system) reduce fall forces and keep the ropes from dragging along the rock, which can slow down movement. Ice climbers favor 60-meter (200-foot) rope lengths, usually with a diameter of 9 millimeters (.4 in) or less, with a water-resistant "dry" coating.

GAITERS: Shell fabric leggings that keep the snow out of your boots.

GLOVES: Waterproof and flexible shell gloves, combined with insulating fleece gloves, keep hands warm and dry.

HARNESS: An ice climbing harness should have adjustable leg loops, multiple gear loops, and the ability to accommodate bulky winter clothing.

ICE SCREWS: These threaded steel tubes twist into solid ice, providing secure anchorage.

INSULATING CLOTHES: Synthetic polyester underwear is the foundation of the winter insulation system. Top this off with fleece layers—jackets, hat, pants, or bibs—that you can put on or take off to accommodate body temperature changes.

SHELL GEAR: Like shingles on a roof, shell jackets and pants fabricated from waterproof, breathable fabrics are the climber's first line of defense against the elements.

In the Swing

Swinging those wicked-looking ice tools at crystalline curtains of ice is the most fun part of the ice climbing game.

ce tools can be frustrating. Not all of us are carpenters, to whom an effortless swing is second nature. But learn these techniques, and remember—practice makes perfect.

SWING IT

Here are a few tips to get the most out of your days on the ice:

X MARKS THE SPOT: Choose a point on the ice. Mark it with an imaginary X, and swing. Your point should be high, but not too high. (You don't want to be overextended.) Look for depressions and weaknesses in the ice surface to maximize pick penetration.

THE WIND UP: Keep your shoulders square to the ice. Draw the tool back while holding the handle with a firm, but not tight, grip until your elbow is bent about 90 degrees.

THE SWING: Using your shoulder, snap the tool forward, keeping your eye on the imaginary X.

THE HIT: Snap your wrist forward at the last second by tightening your hand. If you feel a solid "thunking" sensation vibrate through the tool and into your arm, you've struck a winner.

WHERE'S THE ICE?

Wherever it gets cold and there are cliffs, you'll find ice to climb. Great ice climbing is found in the following areas:

CANADIAN ROCKIES: Arguably the best ice climbing in the world. Alberta and British Columbia have it all: moderate beginner ice climbs, hard sport mixed climbs, and huge ice climbs in an alpine environment.

NORWAY: With cold winter temperatures, huge cliffs, and frozen waterfalls up to 900 feet (279 m) high, Norway is a great place to ice climb.

TETE DE GRAMUSAT, FRANCE: This enormous, steep face offers some of the world's most challenging ice climbs. The frozen north face, with up to 1,100 feet (335 m) of limestone, is draped with ice in a good season.

Cold Fusion

What do you get when you combine cold ice and dry rock? Mixed climbing.

Whether it's climbing a man-made wall in the X Games or desperately hooking thin ice in the Canadian Rockies, mixed climbing is about using everything you've got on snow, ice, and rock.

MIXED-UP

The mixed climber might hook ice tools on rock, twist a pick, or hammer an axe into cracks—all of this is called "drytooling." Edging on tiny ledges with crampons and grabbing an icicle with a gloved hand while swinging an axe at frozen moss with the other are just examples of the surprise challenges that arise in mixed climbing. A mixed route might be 80 feet (24 m) long with massive overhangs, bristling with fixed bolts, and demanding the gymnastic ability of a sport climber as well as the know-how of an ice master. Or a mixed route could be thousands of feet long, set on the flank of a remote and lonely peak, demanding the skills of a high-altitude alpine climber.

MIXED EXPERIENCE

To be a successful mixed climber, you need a strong background in multipitch (scaling more than one pitch in a climb) rock and ice climbing. You also need to know how to judge weather, ice, and snow conditions and other mountain hazards. Whether practiced for the challenge or as training for lofty mountain goals, the mixed game is one of the most engaging and rewarding types of climbing.

MIXED EXTREME: WILL GADD

If there ever was an outdoor, all-around, extreme sports athlete, it's Canadian Will Gadd. Besides being an accomplished trad, sport, and competition climber, Gadd is a leader in modern winter climbing. His groundbreaking mixed climbs in North America and Europe have captured the imagination of a new generation of climbers. Besides establishing the world's hardest ice routes, Gadd is an X Games and World Cup Champion. He won every major international ice climbing competition in 1998 and 1999. A diverse background—Gadd is also a renowned kayaker and skier and has paraglided across America—has instilled an open perspective. "I often think in our quest for harder and higher," he says, "we risk missing the joy of simply moving and being in the mountains."

Alpine Climbing

- Alpinism
- Pack It In
- Himalayan Climbing
- Go Everywhere,
  Do Everything

Despite the cold, the heavy pack, the fear, and the fatigue, there's no place you'd rather be. Welcome to the world of alpine climbing.

Alpinism

Alpinism includes a huge range of activities and requires advanced skills.

Y ou've been climbing since 3:00 A.M. on a ribbon of snow and ice, winding upward into the dark. The world is silent, intensely cold, and pitch black except for the yellow light of your headlamp. Dawn approaches; the gray ribbon hugging the horizon carries the promise of light and warmth. As the red sunrise spreads, you catch a glimpse of the summit thousands of feet above. The vision is breathtaking.

HIGH LIFE

Alpine climbing literally means climbing as if you were in the Alps—the vast mountain range where mountaineering as we know it started. But to mountaineers themselves, alpine climbing stands for a lightweight, self-contained style of climbing over a mixture of glacial terrain, rock, and ice while confronting extreme mountain hazards.

It was from mountaineering that the subsports of climbing were born. It is not a surprise that alpinism draws upon every aspect of the discipline. The skills of rock, big wall, ice, and mixed climbing feed the alpinist's ability to overcome the wide range of mountain challenges.

BEWARE

Some of the hazards you face while alpine climbing might include crevasses and gorges, storms, avalanches, rockfalls, and, in the case of some mountains, high altitude. Alpine climbing is the ultimate adventure and challenge. It's also the most dangerous of all the climbing disciplines, and not to be approached casually—many of the world's most expert climbers have died in pursuit of mountain summits.

Pack It In

The alpinist must deal with every technical challenge imaginable, and do so with a minimum of equipment.

The key to alpinism is keeping it light. Moving fast just isn't possible when you're lugging a huge rack of hardware. Here's some of what you'll need to make it up the mountain.

The author Pete Takeda alpine climbing in the Indian Himalaya.

LIGHT IS RIGHT

The basic hardware needs of the alpine climber are essentially the same as those of the ice or mixed climber. The difference lies in weight. Here are a few examples of the most versatile tools:

CRAMPONS: Spiked metal cages that clip to the bottom of your boots. Semi-rigid models hike well for glacier travel and can handle steep, difficult ice and mixed climbing.

BACKPACK: Simple, sleek lines and the capacity to carry several days' worth of equipment is a must. An alpine pack should move with the body—you'll be climbing with it on your back.

DOUBLE ROPES: Two skinny ropes are less likely to be cut by rockfall than one, and they also allow for long rappels. They come in diameters ranging from 7.6 to 9 millimeters (.3 to .4 in).

HEADLAMP: A reliable headlamp that fits onto your helmet is a must for early-morning alpine starts and late-night climbing.

WIRE GATE CARABINERS: Wire gates are lighter than their solid gate brothers and won't clog with ice and muck.

Crampons

Himalayan Climbing

Climbing in the Himalaya is the dream of most mountaineers.

The soaring altitude, physically debilitating and all too frequently fatal (the terrain above 8,000 meters [26,246 ft] is called "the death zone"), is the defining quality of Himalayan alpinism—no other range is so high.

BIG TOPS

The Himalaya cross several Asian countries, including Pakistan, India, and Nepal. These peaks, the greatest in the world, are home to 14 mountains that top climbing's magic 8,000 m elevation mark. This list includes the world's highest peak, Mount Everest, at 29,035 ft (8,850 m). With countless peaks above 22,965 ft (7,000 m) in elevation, the Himalaya present the ultimate alpine climbing challenges. A noted few mountaineers, such as Tyrolian climbing legend Reinhold Messner, have climbed all fourteen 8,000 m summits.

BE CREATIVE

Perhaps the greatest challenges in the climbing world lie on the flanks of the lower Himalayan summits. The best climbers in the world find their ultimate adventures on the soaring granite big walls, long, extreme, free climbs, and ice-plastered alpine faces of the lower summits of the Himalayan Range.

LAST MAN STANDING

At the end of the 20th century, Slovenian climber Tomaz Humar climbed the huge south face of Dhaulagiri solo. Its 12,000 feet (3,658 m) of extreme Himalayan terrain with 90-degree ice was deemed a "death trap." At 26,794 ft (8,167 m) in elevation, Dhauligiri is the seventh highest mountain in the world. No alpinist in history had combined the challenges of such high altitude with such dangerous and difficult climbing—much less alone.

Perhaps the most striking aspect of Humar's climb is the fact that he turned back just shy of the summit. Exhausted after nine harrowing days on the face, Humar descended. The daring solo was the result of years of practice in which Humar honed his technical skills and vision. But having experienced the deaths of several climbing partners, Humar knew his limits. Looking back, Humar made the right decision. His retreat, despite the temptation of the summit, underlines the fact that no climb is worth dying for.

Go Everywhere, Do Everything

To be a true alpinist, you need to be a well-rounded climber.

Alpine terrain comes in many forms, and a working knowledge of free rock, aid, ice, mixed, and snow climbing is essential.

TRAIN FOR THE TERRAIN

How does the alpinist prepare for the rigors of the mountains? Here are some ideas:

CLIMB ROCK: The best alpinists in the world are accomplished trad, sport, and big wall climbers. Free climbing helps with general conditioning and trains the body and mind in climbing movement and hardware handling. Big wall climbing develops the mental ability to deal with living in the vertical world for days on end. Difficult aid climbing hones the ability to use hardware and equipment to place good anchors where none are in the rock naturally.

CLIMB ICE AND SNOW: Ice is the glue that binds all aspects of alpine climbing. Ice holds the often loose rock of a mountain together. Snow and ice provide the path upon which an alpine climber can move quickly and lightly. To be an alpinist, you will need to be competent with all forms of ice climbing and be familiar and comfortable with everything in the frozen world, from climbing vertical ice to recognizing avalanche hazards.

CLIMB MIXED: The crux of many alpine routes often consists of snow- or ice-covered rock—mixed climbing. Bolt-protected, "sport mixed" climbing provides a convenient method to train for the traditional variety.

BUILD STRENGTH AND STAMINA: Alpinists need to develop strong leg muscles and the endurance to move fast over endless snowfields, glaciers, and trails—often while carrying a heavy pack. Besides just climbing, many alpinists cycle, run, hike, and ski. Crosscountry skiing combines movement in the winter world with an incredible workout. Weight training, treadmill running, and other gym activities help develop power and endurance for those on the run or in the city.

BUILD YOUR MIND: All kinds of climbing demand intense focus. Alpine climbing is no exception. The mountains expose the climber to incredible physical and mental stress and more danger than any other type of climbing. Being alert, aware, and relaxed is a key element in the alpine game. Experience, and the confidence that results from it, comes only after years of mountain adventures.

Climb Smarts

- Climber's Ethics
- Competitive Climbing

You've read the book and you've drooled over the pictures. It's time to get vertical! But climbing is more than just fighting gravity—it's about partnerships, responsibility, and respect for others and the environment.

Climber's Ethics

Take care of yourself—and the rock.

f there was any rule in climbing, it would be, "There are no rules." But when it comes to respecting the environment, there are a few things to keep in mind.

RULES OF THE ROCK

If you are new to the sport, read and follow these rules. If you are already a climber, be a leader and teach "the ropes" to the less experienced.

BE AWARE OF YOUR SURROUNDINGS

- Take the time to find out about local rules and regulations before climbing.
- If possible, climb in less crowded areas and avoid too much impact to the rock.
- Limit the size of your group to no more than 6.

RESPECT THE ENVIRONMENT

- Follow established trails to approach the rock.
- Where no trails exist, use durable ground, such as rock or gravel, and avoid creating new paths.
- Choose a campsite far from surface water, trails, and cliff lines.
- Do not camp at the base of climbs.

USE TOILETS WHERE AVAILABLE

- If there aren't any, urinate away from vegetation, climbing routes, streams, and trails.
- Bring a trowel and dig a hole to dispose of solid human waste. Be sure it's at least 200 feet away from trails, the bases of climbs, water sources, or campsites.
- Put your used toilet paper in resealable plastic bags and carry it in your pack.

LEAVE WHAT YOU FIND

- Avoid trampling the vegetation at bases of climbs and cliff lines.
- Avoid disturbing living things on cliffs (such as plants, salamanders, snakes, and nesting birds).
- Do not cut, prune, or remove trees, shrubs, or vegetation to improve a climb.
- Don't dig or collect artifacts from cliff bases or rock shelters—archaeological sites are protected by federal law.

MINIMIZE USE AND IMPACT OF CAMPFIRES

- Cook on a camp stove instead of a fire; it's quicker, easier, and less harmful.
- If a fire is required, do not make new fire rings; use existing ones instead. Don't build fire rings or pits at the base of any cliff: campfires contaminate cultural resource sites. If you find one, dismantle it and scatter the rocks in a nearby creek.
- Collect only downed and dead wood and only as much as you'll use. Do not cut down live trees or saplings.
- Before you leave, scatter unused wood and make sure the fire is extinguished completely.

MINIMIZE CLIMBING IMPACTS

- Don't chip or create new holds.
- Use removable protection and natural anchors whenever possible.
- Use slings when rappelling from trees instead of wrapping ropes directly around the tree trunk. Choose natural colors for slings if they must be left behind.
- Minimize chalk use, and clean chalk off where you climb.
- Remember, you are in the forest, not a gym. Radios should be left in your car.
- Keep dogs on a leash at all times.

Competitive Climbing

Climbing competitions are as varied as climbing terrain.

Competitions are held indoors and outdoors, on artificial surfaces and natural rock, in the warm sun and on frozen ice. Fun? Very!

473

471

MIND GAMES

Besides being physically taxing, competitive climbing is a mental game. It demands a sharp focus and specialized training, but, as with all aspects of climbing, the best training is to get out there and climb!

GO LOCAL

It doesn't matter how well you climb. To start with, your local gym may hold seasonal competitions open to all age and skill categories. These may involve bouldering—with wild moves and spectacular falls onto huge crash pads—or roped climbing with dramatic arm-pumping cruxes. Your local climbing area may host a seasonal climbing festival with an informal competition. These are not usually about crowning the "best" climber. They are about having lots of fun.

X-ACTLY

Over the last few years, ESPN's X Games have hosted both roped sport and bouldering competitions. The current bouldering craze has made the X Games bouldering competition a real crowd-pleaser. The boulder problems, set by experts, ascend imaginative artificial walls and holds. They are real tests of pure bouldering power. In the world of international climbing competition, the X Games reign as the biggest of the big time. Set your sights high, and you might end up taking the prize in front of screaming fans—broadcast on worldwide television!

In recent years, ice and mixed climbing competitions have become popular. They are held either alongside ice climbing festivals or as part of an international World Cup series on artificial ice structures. Ice festivals are a great place to practice skills and see the experts climb. The world of competition climbing is big and wild! As with climbing itself, there is something for everyone.

Resources

ADDITIONAL INFORMATION ON CLIMBING

BOOKS

Mountaineering: Freedom of the Hills
by Don Graydon, ed
Seattle, WA: Mountaineers Books, 1997

Big Walls
by John Long and John Middendorf
San Ramon, CA: Falcon Books, 1998

Climbing Anchors
by John Long
San Ramon, CA: Falcon Books, 1998

How To Rock Climb (3rd ed.)
by John Long
San Ramon, CA: Falcon Books, 2000

How To Ice Climb!
by Craig Luebben
San Ramon, CA: Falcon Books, 1999

Better Bouldering
by John Sherman
San Ramon, CA: Falcon Books, 1997

Extreme Alpinism
by Mark Twight and James Martin
Seattle, WA: Mountaineers Books, 1999

WEB SITES

Here are some Web sites you can check out to find general information on climbing, climbing groups, and climbing locations.

Access Fund: www.accessfund.org
American Alpine Club: americanalpineclub.org
American Mountain Guides Association: www.amga.com
Climbing (magazine): www.climbing.com
Leave No Trace, Inc.: www.LNT.org
Rock and Ice (magazine): www.rockandice.com

ABOUT THE AUTHOR

Pete Takeda is an author and contributor to numerous publications such as Sports Afield and Vertical. He is Senior Contributing Editor for Climbing magazine, in which he has a regular column, "Pete's Wicked Tales." He is also a member of the Marmot Mountain Ltd. Design Board.

Pete started climbing over 20 years ago in Boise, Idaho. Since then, he's climbed all over the world, from Iceland to India, tackling categories from bouldering, sport, trad, and big wall climbing, to ice, mixed, and Himalayan alpine climbing. He's competed in bouldering, sport, and ice climbing events, including the X Games. Pete lives in Boulder, CO where he is Senior Content Developer for texture/media, a multimedia content and design firm.

PHOTO CREDITS

Design and Editorial: Bill SMITH STUDIO Inc.
Series design: Jay Masoff

EXTREME Sports

CLIMB!

NATIONAL GEOGRAPHIC

**Your Guide to
Bouldering, Sport Climbing,
Trad Climbing, Ice Climbing,
Alpinism, and More.**

BY PETE TAKEDA

Illustrations Jack Dickason

NATIONAL GEOGRAPHIC
WASHINGTON, D.C.

Warning!

Before you read this book you should know that climbing can be dangerous. If you are not careful, and even sometimes if you are, you can break bones, including that hard skull that wraps up your brain. This book explains climbing but is not meant to be used as a training manual. If you plan to climb a mountain (or even a wall at the gym), protect yourself by using the right equipment and by choosing locations and climbs of a difficulty that you're ready for.

A WORD ABOUT HELMETS: Some of the climbers in this book are not wearing helmets. This is a dangerous choice. You should wear a helmet whenever you go climbing. It's your brain—take care of it.

If you do go out and break your head, or any other part of your body or anyone else's body, don't blame National Geographic. We told you to be careful!

(Translation into legalese: Neither the publisher nor the author shall be liable for any bodily harm that may be caused or sustained as a result of conducting any of the activities described in this book.)

One of the world's largest nonprofit scientific and educational organizations, the NATIONAL GEOGRAPHIC SOCIETY was founded in 1888 "for the increase and diffusion of geographic knowledge." Fulfilling this mission, the Society educates and inspires millions every day through its magazines, books, television programs, videos, maps and atlases, research grants, the National Geographic Bee, teacher workshops, and innovative classroom materials. The Society is supported through membership dues, charitable gifts, and income from the sale of its educational products. This support is vital to National Geographic's mission to increase global understanding and promote conservation of our planet through exploration, research, and education.

For more information, please call 1-800-NGS LINE (647-5463) or write to the following address:
National Geographic Society
1145 17th Street N.W.
Washington, D.C. 20036-4688 U.S.A.
Visit the Society's Web site at www.nationalgeographic.com.